LANDSCAPE
DRAWING

Students sometimes begin drawing with set preconceptions about what a drawing should portray and how it should look, and this is particularly true in the case of landscape. In particular, they think that a drawing should provide a copy of the scene they are looking at. However, this is not possible, and any attempt to match reality in this way will not lead to successful or satisfying drawings.

There are many different approaches to drawing the landscape, depending on the feelings, ideas and observations that it provokes in you, and it can be difficult to decide how to set about it, and what to include and what to leave out. The best solution is to break down the subject into its different aspects, and concentrate on just one of them in any one drawing. For example, landscape can be approached by looking at the textures of the different features and finding ways of creating the illusion of those textures by using your materials in different ways. Or you can study the natural elements of atmosphere, water, fire and earth, finding different ways of using your materials to respond to them.

Each chapter tackles a different way of looking at and analysing the landscape, such as through texture, ordering the space or concentrating on your emotional response, and then describes techniques to use for describing that way of looking. By the end, you should have a broad experience that will enable you to work with a number of techniques to express your ideas and feelings. You should work through the projects in the order in which they are given, as later ones build on those in earlier chapters. And by trying out all the approaches described, even if they do not feel quite right for you, you should begin to find out where your strengths and interests lie.

Some of the projects involve drawing for a few hours in the landscape, and in addition to drawing materials you should take suitable clothing for the weather and supplies of food and drinks. It is also important that you are comfortable while working, and a fold-up chair or stool is a definite advantage.

Shape and texture in the landscape

CHAPTER 1

PRECONCEPTIONS

The projects in this chapter involve going into the landscape to make several quick drawings in a sketchbook, using a number of broad-based but mainly gestural techniques. By the end you should have developed confidence in approaching landscape drawing and feel happy about working out of doors, which can be difficult and intimidating for a beginner. The projects should also help you to respond quickly to the environment and enable you to draw, without fear or constraint, in a number of different ways that express your feelings and responses.

The projects have certain conditions attached to them. Some are very quick, with precise times. Others have very specific instructions, such as using both hands. You should comply with these conditions even if they feel strange or restrictive because, as well as trying to break down preconceptions about drawing, the aim of these procedures is to undermine any notions you may have about landscape.

GESTURE

The first seven projects involve gestural drawings, and the attitude that you adopt is crucial to success. A gestural drawing is an action statement. You should allow your eye to scan your field of vision, seeking the primary objects in that field and their position in relation to each other. In other words, you should draw the scene simultaneously with seeing it. It is a fusion of observation and drawing, done quickly, and placing the whole landscape down almost at once. Imagine you have never drawn before and know nothing about it.

MATERIALS

For all the projects in this chapter you need an A4 hardback sketchbook, 3B or 4B pencils or graphite sticks, erasers, pencil sharpener, a watch or clock, something dry to sit on and suitable clothing for the weather, and food and drinks if appropriate.

PROJECT 1
HAND-EYE RELIANCE

Three 5-minute drawings

Do not look at your drawing while drawing.

The aims of this project are to prevent you copying what you see and to help you accept your drawing as an expression or metaphor for what you see. A general misconception is that visual artists should be able to draw 'properly', in the sense of reproducing or making an exact likeness of what they see. This attitude puts a lot of pressure on beginners. In other art forms, artists are applauded for using metaphor. When William Wordsworth wrote *The Daffodils,* he used metaphor to express his feelings.

> I wander'd lonely as a cloud
> That floats on high o'er vales and hills,
> When all at once I saw a crowd,
> A host of golden daffodils.

Wordsworth could have written: I am walking in the hills. I am alone. I have just seen a field with approximately 4000 daffodils in it, and so on. Instead, he chose to use metaphor to describe his experiences and feelings. Unless they are recording something for a specific reason, visual artists do not need to be literal.

Hand-eye reliance

Using pencil or graphite sticks, make three 5-minute drawings. You should be looking at the landscape continuously during this period of drawing, not at your drawing. If your pencil is moving, you should be looking at the subject. You can look at your drawing a couple of times while you work, but not while your pencil is on the paper. This approach should give you a sense of hand-eye co-ordination, as happens when you hit a ball with a bat.

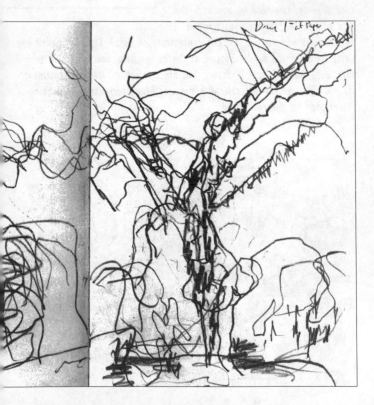

PROJECT 2
GESTURE

Three 5-minute drawings

Using pencil or graphite sticks, do three
5-minute drawings. Fill the page with
each drawing. You need to approach this
with confidence. Imagine your hand is

> *Gesture is a meaningful,
> descriptive scribble and the
> best approach is to draw with
> speed and pressure.*

an extension of your eye. Do not concentrate on detail. Let your pencil line
swing from the top to the bottom of the composition, and from side to
side, until the landscape is drawn. You are creating an artificial statement
for what you see, in this case with gesture. Remember that your drawing is
a metaphor for the real world.

Gesture drawing

PROJECT 3
GESTURE

One 1-minute drawing, one 3-minute drawing, one 5-minute drawing

Each drawing should depict a different view. Speed is of the essence in these drawings. The thought processes that go into drawing and the physical act of doing the drawing must be simultaneous. Trust your reactions. This can be difficult at first because we respond to most things in life in a more controlled, calculated way, taking time to reflect, whereas in this drawing you should be spontaneous.

PROJECT 4
UNFAVOURED HAND

Three 10-minute drawings

Work using the same approach as in the previous project. Make three 10-minute drawings using your unfavoured hand: if you are right-handed use your left hand, and vice versa. The movements of your favoured hand are rooted in habit, and you need to break this in order to progress. The unfavoured hand will open up new opportunities and allow you to be more expressive and less predetermined.

PROJECT 5
USING BOTH HANDS

Three 5-minute drawings

Again, work in a gestural way. In this drawing, use both hands simultaneously. Let one hand start the drawing at one side of the picture while the other hand starts on the other side. Begin to draw, but do not move each hand in the same direction. Make each hand draw in different directions, working on different parts of the drawing. Let your hands cross over so that they both draw on both sides of the picture.

PROJECT 6
CONTINUOUS LINE

Three 5-minute drawings

Place your pencil or graphite stick on the paper and associate this with a point in the landscape. Look around the location, scanning it and observing the features. Co-ordinate this with the movement of your hand to make the drawing. As you draw, compare and locate points in the landscape in relation to each other, establishing rough proportons in this search. Do not take the pencil off the paper while you are drawing.

Try to make the line appear as though it is travelling through space, indicating depth in the scene by varying the pressure on the pencil at appropriate points. If you want something to appear near, make the mark darker and thicker. If you want something to appear in the distance, make the mark lighter and thinner. As the line moves through the air from one point to another, imagine that it is a bird flying from tree to tree, leaving the line as a trace of its movements. At the same time, try to make spatial sense of the trace so that it moves through and activates the depth of field.

Continuous-line drawing

HOLDING THE PENCIL

Three 5-minute drawings

We readily pick up a pencil in the same way, holding it as we have held it thousands of times before, never questioning this procedure or the limitations that it forces on us. However, by holding the pencil as for writing, you restrict the flow of the drawing as you can only move the hand and wrist. Instead, think of ways to make marks using other parts of the body. Each provides a new, exciting experience that will also bring about a different sense of control, scale and expression. Here are a few suggestions, but try to think of others ways to evolve a drawing.

Hold the pencil like a dagger. This brings the action of the whole arm into the making of a drawing.

Hold the pencil right at the end, between thumb and forefinger. This limits the drawing action and the pressure that you can apply.

Hold the pencil in your mouth. This brings the movement of the head and torso into the drawing.

Place the sketchbook on the ground. Take off a shoe and sock and hold the pencil between your toes. The whole balance of the body is brought into this drawing.

SILHOUETTE

One 10-minute drawing

This drawing is done more slowly than the gestural drawings. It is considered rather than spontaneous. Look for a landscape that has a foreground, a middle ground, and a background that meets the sky at the horizon. You should also look for objects in the foreground, such as a tree or building, that overlap the middle ground and background and break though the horizon line. Look for similar objects in the middle ground that overlap the background and the horizon line. This overlap creates the illusion of space.

The aim is to draw the silhouettes of the objects and the way they link up with other objects in the same plane. Effectively, you are drawing the shape of objects, both positively and negatively.

Start with the background. The first stage is to draw the horizon line and the silhouettes of all parts of objects that are above the horizon line from your viewpoint. Starting at the edge of the paper, draw the horizon line until you meet the first object that protrudes above it. Draw up and over this object until your pencil returns to the horizon line. Then continue to draw along the horizon line until you come to the next object that protrudes above it; draw up and over this object until you return to the horizon line. Continue with this until you reach the other edge of the paper. You have now effectively cut the paper in two (Step 1).

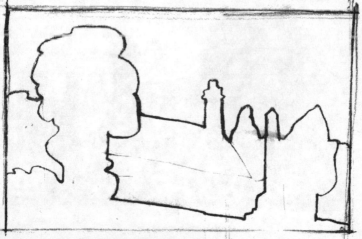

Silhouette drawing, Step 1

Silhouette drawing, Step 2

Planal recession

The next stage is to draw the middle ground, linking it to the horizon line with objects that overlap, drawing the silhouettes of all parts of objects that are below the horizon line from your viewpoint.

Put your pencil on the original starting point on the horizon line and begin to draw along that line again until you come to the point where you meet the first object. This time take the line down around the object until it meets the ground. Then continue this line along the ground, returning back to the edge of the paper (below your original starting point on the horizon line). Now find where the other side of this object touches the horizon line. Begin to draw down this side of the object until you come to the point where it meets the ground, and follow this line up and over other objects as they appear either to meet the horizon line again or to go out of the other side of the picture. Do the same with the other objects that overlap the horizon line.

Continue in this way until you have established the three areas of background, middle ground and foreground (Step 2).

PROJECT 9

PLANAL RECESSION

One ¹/₂-1 hour drawing

Planal recession means creating the illusion of different planes (like flat sheets of card) overlapping each other and appearing to go back in space.

This is very similar to the last project, and you could use the last example as a basis for this drawing, as you have already created planal recession through the use of the overlap. The aim here is to emphasise recession by using tone.

First, make the foreground area a very dark tone. Then make the middle ground area a slightly lighter tone, and the background area a very light tone. This will help the illusion of space and depth. You can leave the sky white or make it dark from the horizon line to the top of the paper, or the reverse.

You can play with the tone combinations to see how they affect the idea of depth and space.

PROJECT 10
MEMORY

One 1/2-hour drawing

We are continuously using our memories when drawing. The only situation when we do not is when using hand-eye reliance. In every drawing, even though it may only be for a fraction of a second, as you turn your head away from the scene back to your drawing you are using your memory. This project extends the ideas of memory.

Look at your landscape subject continuously for 10 minutes, assessing the composition. What objects are in the scene and where are they positioned? How do they relate to each other and the space they occupy? Assess the light: how is it falling on the landscape and what effect is it having? You can also take into account things such as texture (see 'Landscape Textures'). When you have completed your observations, start a drawing of what you remember without making any further reference to the scene. Spend about 20 minutes on the drawing itself. When you have finished, compare the drawing with the original view.

Try to develop your memory skills as this will be useful in later drawings. It will also allow you to be less reliant on drawing from observation all the time. Eventually, good memory skills will enable you to use more artistic licence in your work.

PROJECT 11
REDUCED LINES

One 20-minute drawing

First make a continuous line drawing as in Project 6. Then break this line by rubbing out sections in order to reduce the number of lines needed to describe the scene in front of you. First, use only ten lines. From that drawing, try to reduce the number of lines to seven, and so on until you are down to three lines, or even one. Throughout, do not lose the essence of what you are describing.

Reduced-line drawing

CHAPTER 2

LANDSCAPE TEXTURES

Touch is a sense that we all possess, yet we often take it very much for granted. We are constantly using touch, and, even if at an unconscious level, we are being made aware all the time of our immediate textural environment. This experience is automatically stored in the mind for future reference, and we can very easily access our memory of textural information.

Artists throughout history and across cultures have been fascinated by the challenge of recreating a sense of touch. Whether consciously or unconsciously, their focus has been pulled towards the surface qualities of the scene portrayed. Texture may not have been the primary concern of the artist, but that did not stop them trying to excel at describing it. There are many good examples, but the following, in particular, will help you to understand the issues raised in this chapter: the drawings by the Chinese artist Xu Xi (c.1020-90) of early spring and winter landscapes; mountain landscapes, studies of rocks, a storm, water and eddies, and numerous studies of plants by Leonardo da Vinci (1452-1519); studies of trees by Titian (d. 1576); the landscapes of Pieter Breughel the Elder (c.1525-69) and Rembrandt (1606-69); and the landscape and seascape drawings of Vincent van Gogh (1853-90). Max Ernst (1891-1976) invented dream-like textural landscapes. All these drawings have great intensity expressed through variation in mark-making. They are also visually exciting drawings that can hold the viewer's attention.

The experience and understanding of mark-making that the following projects provide should enable you to create landscape drawings that express texture, surface, space and form. The projects provide a number of clear procedures to give confidence in drawing the landscape using a textural approach, and in mark-making through experimenting with different mediums. They involve some closely observed individual studies of the different types of objects encountered in the landscape, a more complete study of the landscape that expresses the texture, space and form observed there, and frottage used to construct a landscape drawing.

PROJECT 1

DEVELOPING MARK-MAKING

1-2 hours
Materials: *sketchbook, pencils, graphite sticks, charcoal, compressed charcoal, inks and dip pens, felt-tip pens, erasers, and any other drawing material you want to work with*

You need to know what your medium is capable of in terms of mark-making. Far too often, people take things for granted, in particular the way in which they hold the drawing tool and how they use it. Because of this, they persistently make the same statement. This project demands that you break with these ingrained habits and develop your own vocabulary of marks. Endeavour to make an inventory of marks that you can refer to later — like a dictionary divided into sections: one for pencil marks, one for graphite marks, one for charcoal marks and so on.

For example: take the charcoal and, instead of drawing with the end to make a line, place it flat on its side and pull it down the paper. Notice what a fine, tight line this makes. Lay the charcoal on the paper in the same way and drag it sideways; look at the different impression made. Repeat the process again, but this time instead of dragging the charcoal, twist it as though you were using a compass. There are many more ways in which to develop and use the medium. Think of making as varied a collection of statements as possible: fluid marks, rigid marks, dark marks, light marks, hard marks and soft marks. Position these experiments on the paper so that you have marks next to each other that create an obvious contrast. And think about how you hold the drawing tool to make your marks. Be open in your attitude and approach towards this and try different methods. This research will enable you to broaden and develop your mark-making and prepare you for the next two projects.

Right: Examples of mark-making

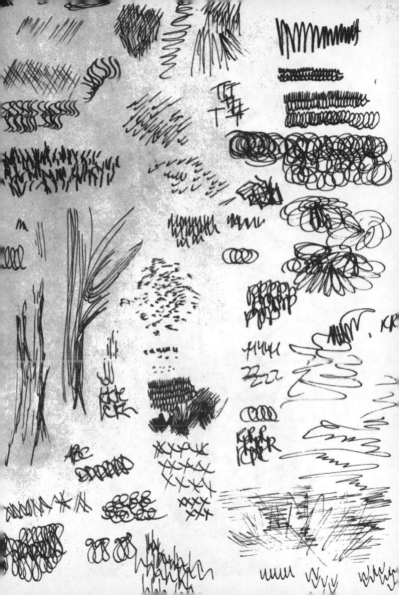

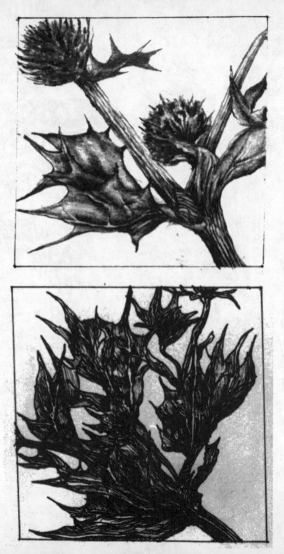

PROJECT 2
CLOSE-UP STUDIES OF NATURE

Each study no longer than 30 minutes
Materials: *A1 paper, any of the drawing materials used in Project 1*

Having done some research in mark-making, you should be ready to attempt a close-up drawing from Nature. Go into the landscape and collect examples to bring home and draw. It is usually possible to find various fungi, a broken branch with interesting bark, a thistle and so on. If you live near the sea, you can scour the beaches for interesting textural objects.

Select an object and lay it on a neutral ground, such as a piece of white paper. Observe and analyse this object closely, becoming very familiar with what it looks like. You need to understand its form and texture, and how that texture is constructed. Once you have sufficient understanding of the subject, you can think about how to draw it.

Observe closely. Understand your observations, and analyse how the object is texturally constructed. Then draw that understanding, not the literal observation. For example, if you are drawing a piece of wood, the grain of the wood should echo its form. It would not just lie flat over the surface (unless, of course, the surface is flat).

In the first part of the drawing, you should deal with the structure of the object. Use line to describe the basic proportions and to give a sense of the underlying fundamental form. For example, the fundamental form of a thistle-head is a sphere. Use cross-sectional analysis to describe the form. Not all objects will have an obvious form: if you are drawing a flat object such as a leaf, you would not draw the form but the shape, and then proceed to imply the texture within that shape.

Left: Close-up textural studies of natural objects

Draw the object larger than life-size. This will make your drawing easier and less fiddly. Once you have drawn the basic outline, begin to put in the different textures. Students often make the mistake of including every detail that they see. If you do this, however, your drawing will soon become laborious and uninteresting. A certain type of concentration and understanding are required for this drawing. You need to draw a textural metaphor; that is, you need to invent a visual language of marks to describe what you see and understand.

First draw objects individually; then together, to give textural comparisons.

PROJECT 3
STUDIES OF OBJECTS IN THE LANDSCAPE

Each study no longer than 30 minutes
Materials: *A4 hardback sketchbook, pencils, graphite sticks, pencil sharpener, erasers, felt-tip pens, pen and inks (not charcoal or compressed charcoal because they are too cumbersome on a small page)*

The aim is to select individual objects within the landscape to draw, and to make studies of these objects as with the objects that you took home.

Choose an object, for example a tree. Draw it in isolation on the sketchbook page, making a textural observation of it. Use the methods described in the previous project to approach these studies. In your sketchbook, continue to experiment with different ways of making marks, as you did in Project 1. You should become gradually more familiar with the elements that occupy your chosen landscape. Look at the landscape drawings of John Constable (1776-1837) and his studies of clouds, Titian's studies of trees and Leonardo's studies of water running around a post. Make lots of studies, as this will broaden your textural experience and give you the confidence to approach the next drawing, a full landscape.

Right: Textural study of an object in the landscape

MAKING A WINDOW-MOUNT

A window-mount helps you to frame and organise your composition. You can buy plastic versions with a grid printed on one side, but you can quickly make one out of A4 paper.

Take an A4 sheet of paper. Draw a line from one corner to the diagonally opposite corner. Repeat this with the other two corners. This finds the centre point of the paper (Step 1).

From the centre point, draw a horizontal line and a vertical line to form four rectangles (Step 2).

Subdivide the four rectangles in the same way (Step 3).

This gives you a central rectangle which will be in proportion to your A1 sheet of paper. Cut out this rectangle, and you have a window-mount with four measuring marks along the top, bottom and sides around the edges of the window (Step 4).

Step 1

Step 2

Step 3

Step 4

USING A WINDOW-MOUNT

You can select a composition by looking through the window-mount. If you are right-handed use your left hand to hold the window-mount, and vice versa if you are left-handed. Always look through the mount from the same position.

PROJECT 4
THE LANDSCAPE

One 5-hour drawing
Materials: *A2 hardback sketchbook, pencils, graphite sticks, pencil sharpener, erasers, felt-tip pens, pen and inks, charcoal or compressed charcoal, window-mount*

> *Remember that you are making a metaphor for texture, not drawing literally from observation.*

You are going to draw a selected part of the landscape and you will be in this position for some time, so it is essential to be comfortable.

Use the window-mount to choose your composition, and begin to draw the outline of the objects within it. While doing this, you should establish the relationship of the objects to each other, in space and proportions, so that you have the basic layout. Now start to deal with the main issue – texture. Begin to draw the contrasting textures that the landscape and the objects within it imply. Think back to the mark-making project, and on another page in your sketchbook make experimental marks that could be used in this drawing.

The difference between this and the previous drawing is one of context. Each object is drawn both in space and in context with the other objects, rather than in isolation. The way that you draw texture should work not only texturally, but should also imply spatial understanding. For example, if you are drawing the bark of a tree close to you, and you are also drawing the same type of tree further away, you can use the same mark for both trees, but the scale and weight of the marks should be different. The scale of the mark in the distance should be smaller and lighter in tone than the scale of the mark for objects close to you. This drawing is quite intense, and needs a lot of attention and concentration, so be prepared for a long session.

Overleaf: Textural landscape drawing

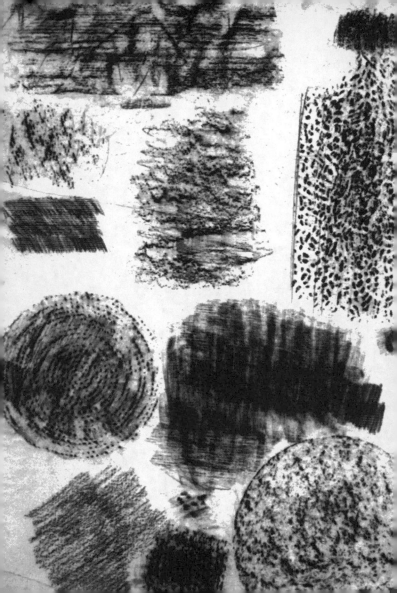

PROJECT 5
FROTTAGE AND COLLAGE

One 5-hour drawing
Materials: *about 12 sheets of A1 newsprint paper, A1 cartridge paper, graphite sticks, or charcoal, or compressed charcoal, water-based glue (PVA), brush*
In this project you are going to construct a collage landscape using frottage.

Gather a lot of examples of frottage on newsprint. Go around the house and out of doors, taking impressions from any textured surface by laying the paper over the surface and scribbling on the paper with a pencil or other drawing material. This gives the impression of the texture underneath. Make these areas of frottage quite large — about half a page of newsprint each. Whichever medium you start with, such as graphite (which works particularly well for this), stay with it for the whole project. Make different types of textures, as you are going to use them to construct a landscape.

Take an A1 piece of cartridge paper and draw the plan of a landscape on it. You can do this at home using a landscape drawing from your sketchbook. Once you have this plotted out, cut and tear the frottage pieces and begin to stick them down on the landscape in appropriate places (illustrated overleaf). Select frottage that is appropriate for the area that it is describing. For instance, when doing tree bark, select frottage that you think best describes that tree bark. Also, as you arrange the collage, try to emphasise contrasts in textures, both in scale and in weight of mark, so that they create a spatial and textural metaphor for the landscape.

Always start from the furthest point in the landscape because, as you build forwards, you will enhance the sense of space by the physical action of overlapping. You can do any number of these drawings.

Left: Examples of frottage
Overleaf: A collage landscape using frottage

CHAPTER 3

CLASSICAL SPACE

The way in which artists have used landscape can be roughly divided into two approaches. From the classical tradition are those artists who impose order on and look for order in the landscape. From another tradition, the romantic school, are those artists who render the landscape through a more naturalistic interpretation. This and the following chapter look at ways to organise and analyse the landscape based on the classical sense of order.

The classical artist Claude Lorraine (1600-82) always referred to an underlying composition in landscape. This involved a foreground with a dark mass, usually a temple or a mass of trees, to one side, casting a shadow over this front plane. The foreground is where the human activity usually takes place and is the focal point of the picture. The eye then moves back through the picture space to the middle ground. About two-thirds across the picture in the middle ground there would be another feature, usually a group of trees. The eye is then taken back through another two planes. The first possibly being occupied by another group of trees and the last plane by distant mountains and a city. Claude used a number of other devices, such as bridges, rivers or cattle fording a stream, to help the sense of space and composition. However, perhaps the most important device that he used for creating space was tone. He created the illusion of recession within the picture space through a very dark yet clear foreground leading to a light, atmospheric background.

You will not be using as complicated a system as Claude's, but you should use some of these devices and apply them to your observations. The aims of the projects are to help you organise the compositional space in a drawing, to analyse and structure a drawing, and to abstract a composition with a sense of order.

To be successful with this approach, you need to be the type of artist who tends towards the analytical rather than the emotive. Those who are more expressive will enjoy the last two chapters. However, there is no reason why you should not attempt this way of working, as it just might inform you of new ways to express your ideas, feelings and responses. Before tackling the projects, look at the work of classical landscape artists such as Nicolas Poussin ((1593/4-1665) and Claude. Study how they constructed their work using the basic analysis above. Also look at the work of Paul Cezanne (1839-1906), Georges Seurat (1859-91), Lyonel Feininger (1871-1956) and Piet Mondrian (1872-1944).

PROJECT 1
A LANDSCAPE CONSTRUCTED WITH TONE

One 5-hour drawing
Materials: *A3 hardback sketchbook, 3B or 4B pencils or graphite sticks, erasers, pencil sharpener, window-mount*

A landscape constructed with tone

In this project you are going to record and order a scene, rather than render it in its natural state. In the next project, you will use this research to construct a landscape drawing, using tone to create form and space.

You need to select the type of landscape that lends itself to a classical composition. Do not pick wild or overgrown scenery such as moorland. Look instead for a landscape that has been influenced by human activity, such as farmland, a stately home or gardens. The grounds around stately homes provide the perfect landscape for this project as they are not only ordered, but often harbour follies in the classical style.

Having selected a place to work, compose the picture using the window-mount. You need not draw exactly what is in front of you; you can re-order

A landscape constructed with tone

it to create a balanced and harmonious composition. Objects can be moved within the composition to give a clearer sense of order. For example, you might decide to move a clump of trees to the right or left. Think about how the Claude landscapes were composed and base your thinking on this. It is a good idea to have some examples of Claude's work with you for reference. Remember that the landscape should have clear foreground and middle ground, and the distance should contain the horizon line. Begin by drawing these areas in silhouette using line (see 'Preconceptions', Project 8). Then draw in any elements, such as trees, fences, rock formations and houses within the shapes of the silhouettes.

The next stage is to lay down the fundamental tones or tonal base. Still following the rules of Claude, start by making the whole of the foreground the darkest tone. The middle ground should be a shade or two lighter, and

the background the lightest tone, leaving the sky white. You have now established the tonal base and created spatial recession on the picture plane. Next, begin to refine the drawing, using tone to describe the objects within the space in more detail. Observe how light hits the form of objects in the landscape, and then use this as a means of describing and creating the forms, by modelling the objects with light.

You can use the natural light source, but this is continually changing and can create confusion in a drawing of this nature. Instead, you can invent a directional light source for each plane to emphasise the form. For example, the foreground could have an imagined light source illuminating all the objects within that plane from the right, whereas the middle ground could have an imagined light source illuminating all the objects within that plane from the left or the front. Draw all the objects within each plane, modelling every object clearly with its imagined light source. When you have completed a number of these drawings, you should have a group of drawings that you can reconstruct on a larger scale at home.

PROJECT 2

SCALING UP A LANDSCAPE DRAWING

One 5-hour drawing
Materials: *A0 paper, pencils, charcoal, erasers, pencil sharpener, A3 sketch from the previous project or a black-and-white copy of a Claude or Poussin landscape, 1m (3ft) straight-edge or ruler*

One way to develop drawings done directly from Nature is to scale them up, using a grid, to A0 size, or A1 if you do not have much space. This project works much better at the A0 size, so only use A1 if absolutely necessary. If you want to gain confidence with this type of work you could start with a black-and-white copy of a painting by Claude or Poussin, scaling this up and working from it.

Carefully tear an A3 sketch from Project 1 out of your sketchbook and place it in the corner of the A0 or A1 paper (Step 1). Use a pencil to draw the grid. Draw a diagonal line through the sketch and extend it to the opposite corner of the large sheet (Step 2). Where the extended line meets the top edge of the paper, draw a vertical line (Step 3).

This will give you the proportions of your original sketch, although in this

Scaling-up a drawing

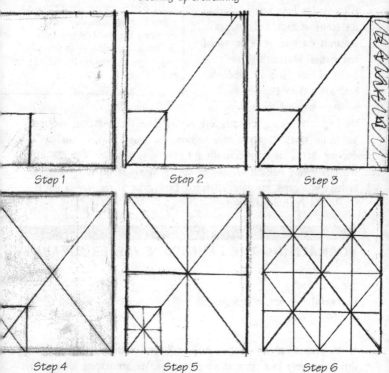

Step 1   Step 2   Step 3

Step 4   Step 5   Step 6

case the A3 sketch should be the same proportions as the A0 or A1 paper. Tear or cut off any waste.

The next stage is to grid up both the original sketch and the drawing paper. On the original sketch and on the large sheet of paper, draw a diagonal line between the other two corners (Step 4). You have now established the centre of each, and you can construct the grid. Draw horizontal and vertical lines through the centre of both (Step 5). Subdivide both again (Step 6).

> ### AO PAPER
> You may be able to buy a sheet of AO paper. If not, you can join two sheets of A1. Butt two sides together without any overlap and stick a strip of masking tape all along the join. The side with masking tape will be the back of the drawing. If the paper is too large to use on your drawing board, attach it to a wall.

Next, map out the drawing on the large sheet, using charcoal. Use line to place the landscape, and then put in the tone. When you have finished, you should have a scaled-up drawing that is far more dramatic than the original sketch. You can make this into a true classical drawing by adding figures in the foreground, perhaps with some anecdotal reference. Look again at the way in which Claude and Poussin used figures.

PROJECT 3

FORMALISING THE LANDSCAPE (AFTER CEZANNE)

One 3-hour drawing
Materials: *A3 hardback sketchbook, 3B or 4B pencils or graphite sticks, erasers, pencil sharpener, window-mount*

In this project you are going to look at Nature in its raw state, and from that create your own sense of intrinsic order. We are leaping forward from

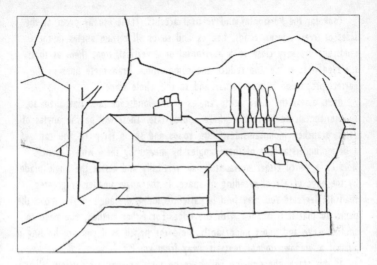

Formalising the landscape, Step 1

the 18th century of Claude to the 20th century to examine the attitudes of Cezanne and Seurat towards the landscape. Before starting, look at the work of Cezanne and Seurat — in particular Cezanne, who was the richer and more abundant of the two. Cezanne's compositions are made up of straight lines rather than following the natural curves of the landscape. The horizontals, verticals and angled vectors to which Cezanne reduced his compositions are the scaffolding on which his work hangs.

A rural landscape that still possesses a raw, natural look is better for this project than one that has been organised by humans. For example, a series of farm buildings next to a natural feature such as an outcrop of rock, or worked land that edges onto untamed land. The space in the landscape should echo the classical idea of space, with a foreground, middle ground and background, but in a more natural setting.

Look for the horizontal and vertical accents. These usually occur at the sides of trees, houses, roads, hedges and so on. If certain angles in the landscape are very close to a horizontal or a vertical, treat them as that; the idea is to refine and reduce the composition. Draw these lines in the correct proportion to each other and to the whole scene.

Next, assess the more acute angles in the landscape, and link them to the horizontals and verticals where appropriate. These will be the angles of roofs, branches, mountainsides, hills, roads and so on (Step 1). You can get a better understanding of these angles by measuring them with a pencil. Hold up a pencil either horizontally or vertically and assess the angle made by the edge of a roof receding in space. Is the angle smaller or greater than 45 degrees? You may find it easier to judge the angle if you move the pencil so that it is aligned with the edge. For either method, you need to shut one eye and, most importantly, hold the pencil as if you are holding it against a window; do not twist it away from you.

At this stage, the drawing will have no form or spatial recession. What you have on the drawing surface is the scaffolding on which to build the rest of it. The next step is to create the illusion of space (Step 2). You have created a number of edges and planes in relationship to each other. It is these edges and planes that you need to work on to construct the idea of spatial recession, using shading on either the inside or the outside of an edge. For instance, if you are applying this system to shading the planes of a building, the plane that recedes into the picture space should be shaded at the edge where it meets the plane that is in front of it. This system brings some edges of planes forwards and sends others slightly back in space, and allows the eye to move back through the picture space.

This is a very regimented way of producing a drawing, but you can play around with these ideas, abstracting them further. Look at early Cubist work to see how these ideas were developed.

Right: Formalising the landscape, Step 2

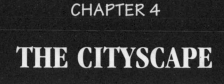

CHAPTER 4

THE CITYSCAPE

C ities and towns have played a significant but usually secondary role in art. Like other landscape subjects, cityscapes were used as a device to contain an important event such as a religious, historic or poetic scene. They were either based on realistic cities, recording the architecture of the time, or they would be cityscapes of fantasy aspiring to the classical or divine. Cityscapes were also often combined with the natural but ordered landscapes of the classical ideal.

As the city or town has been designed, created and conceived by human rather than natural forces, this type of landscape has its own intrinsic order. By its very nature, this subject lends itself to a structured way of working. Before starting to draw a cityscape, you must deal with the inherent order of the subject, and the approach adopted in the following projects is a formal one, using theory to realise and present observations. Nevertheless, many artists have depicted the city very successfully without using a formal approach (covered in 'The Natural Landscape' and 'Expressionism').

In this chapter we look at the basic theory of perspective. This will enable you to approach and demonstrate drawings of towns and cities from observation, to abstract compositions from your observations, and to make drawings that have a sense of order, harmony and balance.

Before starting, look at Leonardo's studies of perspective for his *Adoration of the Magi*, *The Stonemason's Yard* by Canaletto (1697-1768) and the architectural drawings of Antonio Sant'Elia (1888-1916).

PERSPECTIVE DRAWING OF A STREET FROM OBSERVATION

One 3-4 hour drawing
Materials: *A3 sketchbook, a range of pencils, erasers, window-mount*

This project is based on some basic rules of perspective. First, choose your location. You need to select a place that contains perspectival depth, such as a street that recedes into the distance from your viewpoint. If possible, choose one that contains a simple block of terraced houses. Choose a simple composition rather than a complicated cityscape for this first drawing, as this will make the rules of perspective easier to understand.

Buildings

Use the window-mount to select a composition. Include four or five houses receding into the distance and ignore the rest of the view. Treat this block of houses in isolation. Make sure that the roofs and bases of the houses are included. The composition should have a definite starting point in the foreground, such as the corner of a building. With a simple block of houses, this point of departure should be self-evident. Although there is nothing wrong with taking another starting point, by starting with a building in the foreground you can establish the rest of the drawing from this point. Once you have started, continue to draw from the same position and viewpoint throughout, otherwise the drawing will become very distorted.

Draw a vertical line depicting the corner of the first building, bearing in mind where it is positioned when seen through the window-mount, and make this line the correct height and proportion in relation to the window-mount and your paper. This is your first measurement. It will be a bench-

Right: Perspective drawing of buildings from observation

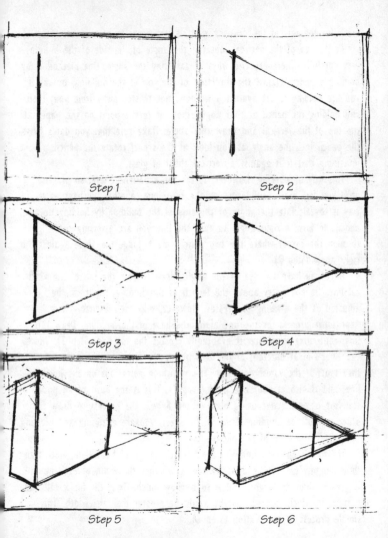

Step 1

Step 2

Step 3

Step 4

Step 5

Step 6

mark for the rest of the drawing so it is important to be accurate (Step 1).

At the top of the vertical, observe the angle of the side of the building very carefully. There are two ways of assessing the angle. One method is by holding a pencil against the direction of the top of the building, but as if you are holding it flat against a window, not twisted away from you; then, still holding the pencil at that angle, move it to the point on the paper at the top of the vertical and draw this angle. Make sure that you don't twist the pencil into the angle as you look at the scene; rotate the pencil, imagining that it is against a vertical sheet of glass.

This way of working, however, is for the experienced eye, so practise until you feel more confident with the technique. Another, perhaps easier, way is to calculate the angle of the side of the building by holding up two pencils to form a right angle so that the line you are assessing cuts through the corner where the two pencils meet. Judge the angle against the right angle (Step 2).

Once you have an idea of the angle, draw it from the top of the vertical line. Do not worry about the length of this line yet, as it can be adjusted as the drawing progresses. However, make it reasonably long. Repeat the process for the line along the base of the building. Draw this line, continuing it so that it eventually crosses the top line (Step 3). These two lines run at different angles and ultimately converge. The point where they cross is the vanishing point. The vanishing point falls on the horizon line, and is also at your eye level (Step 4). This is the basis of an understanding of perspective using observation. Repeat the process to draw the other side of the building (Step 5). In effect, you are analysing and plotting the angles and lines of perspective.

The next step is to find the depth of the block of houses in relation to their height. This can be done by seeing whether the width of each house is greater than its height, and if so by how much. Or is the block tall and narrow, in which case the height would be greater than the width. This is a simple process of observation (Step 6).

Architectural details

You now have the basic form of the building, and you can begin to embellish it with architectural details such as windows, doors and roofs. This can be done using the same system of measuring angles as for the top and bottom of the buildings, or with a more mathematical procedure that involves dividing the sides of the building to give a perspectival and proportional framework within which to place the other elements. It looks rather technical, but it trains your eye in the understanding of perspectival recession.

Start with the largest facade of the building, which is a rectangle going back in space. You are going to subdivide this rectangle using a system that produces what appear to be a number of Union Jacks within it. First, draw a diagonal line from one corner to the opposite corner. Do the same between the other two corners. This creates a cross within the rectangle that gives its perspectival centre (Step 1). Draw a vertical line through the centre point from the top to the bottom of the rectangle. Then draw in the next

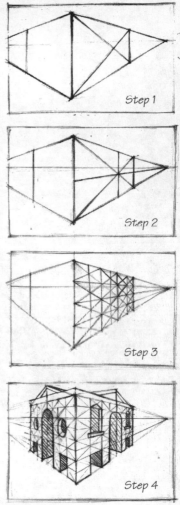

Step 1

Step 2

Step 3

Step 4

Architectural details

49

Observed perspective drawing of a street

> In this drawing you have applied a theory, or drawing system, developed from your own observations. However, theory is for weaker moments; it can prove a dangerous crutch to lean on. This process of drawing is very mechanical, and you need to bring your own creative mark into the drawing. When you become more familiar with perspective and can use it without thinking, you will be able to make a more confident and personal type of line.

perspective line using the centre point in the rectangle and the vanishing point. This should produce a Union Jack motif within the rectangle (Step 2). Continue this process until you have a detailed enough framework on which to add architectural detail (Step 3). All you need do now is to calculate how and where features such as doors and windows fit into this framework (Step 4). Repeat the process on the other side of the building.

Try a number of drawings using this system to familiarise yourself with the procedure, and gradually impose your own identity on the drawings.

PROJECT 2

PERSPECTIVE DRAWING OF A CITYSCAPE FROM OBSERVATION

One 3-4 hour drawing
Materials: *A3 sketchbook, a range of pencils, erasers, window-mount*

Now that you are more familiar and confident with perspective, you can embark on a drawing that takes in a full view of the cityscape rather than just one street (illustrated overleaf). Use the window-mount to select an interesting perspectival composition. Use the same system as in the previous project; that is, assess the angles from the verticals for each individual building. Some buildings, especially if they are in the same street, are in the same orientation, but others will be in a different orientation.

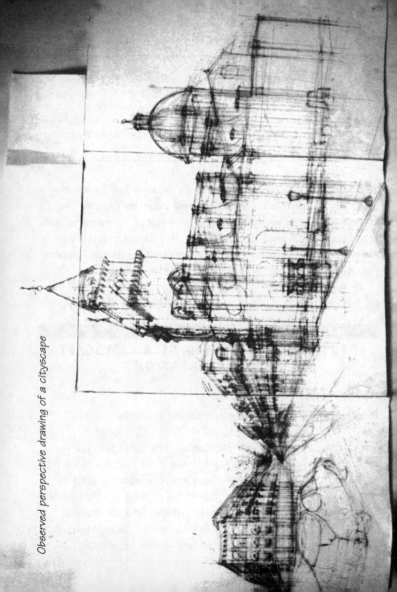

Observed perspective drawing of a cityscape

PROJECT 3

ABSTRACTION AND ORDER

Two drawings, 3-4 hours
Materials: *A3 sketchbook or A1 paper, a range of pencils, erasers*

You need not go outside for this drawing; instead, you can base it on drawings from the preceding projects.

Abstraction and order, Drawing 1

Before starting, look at the work of Lyonel Feininger and Piet Mondrian. Feininger used the angles of buildings by extending them to create a flat, yet dynamic, picture space. Mondrian reduced the elements of the cityscape to their basic essence, using only variations on the vertical and horizontal accents in the composition to give a pure state of proportion, which in turn creates a sense of harmony.

In the first drawing, take the perspectival directions or vectors of buildings and extend them. Do the same with the horizontal and vertical lines. This will create an unusual web of lines that, in turn, create a series of shapes across the picture plane. The next step is to create the illusion of an invented space by using shading at the edges of shapes. Where an edge is shaded, the shaded part will recede and the unshaded part will appear to come forward. At this stage, you can develop the drawing however you want. Try to find your own intrinsic sense of space and proportion. Play around with this type of drawing: you will probably enjoy the freedom of composing a drawing without the responsibility of representation.

The second drawing involves simplifying the composition even further. This drawing should be based purely on horizontal and vertical lines, as in Mondrian's work. You can use all the horizontals and verticals in your original drawing; put them down keeping the same proportions. The next step is to decide whether the angled lines are closer to the vertical or the horizontal. Then draw them as horizontals or verticals. Next, decide how to make the drawing into an interesting statement. You can imply a sense of space using scale, weight of mark, overlap and so on. Again, the drawing is now in a state for you to organise and develop in your own way.

All the projects in this chapter have been based on technical processes, and ultimately you must bring into the work your own identity, ideas and feelings about this way of working. Otherwise, the work will go no further than demonstrating method or theory.

Right: Abstraction and order, Drawing 2

CHAPTER 5

THE NATURAL LANDSCAPE

Since the 1650s, landscape has increasingly been seen as something beautiful in its own right. As human understanding of the Universe grew, Nature did not seem so threatening. Artists were inspired by the natural view rather than by the ordered scene, and people became more responsive to the pleasure that spectacular scenery provided. As a result, a more naturalistic approach to the landscape in art became increasingly popular.

In northern Europe, artists such as Jacob van Ruisdael (1628/29-82) and Meindert Hobbema (1638-1709) began to render the landscape in a natural, unordered manner with windswept skies and shadows on the ground cast by clouds. These artists and their ideas were a major influence on British landscape artists such as John Constable (1776-1837), who in turn influenced French artists, in particular the School of the Barbizon, which included Théodore Rousseau (1812-67), Jean-Baptiste-Camille Corot (1796-1875) and Gustave Courbet (1818-77). Meanwhile, Constable's great rival J.M.W. Turner (1775-1851) greatly influenced Impressionist painters such as Claude Monet (1840-1926), Alfred Sisley (1839-99) and Camille Pissaro (1830-1903). Turner, who was himself influenced by Claude, excelled at describing and expressing the elements and the landscape in their fullest glory.

Before starting the projects, study Turner's work. In particular, look at *Rain, Steam and Speed*, *Snow Storm*, *Steam Boat off a Harbour Mouth*, *Norham Castle Sunrise*, *Peace Burial at Sea*, *Sunset at Rouen* and *The Burning of the Houses of Parliament*. These pictures deal with the elements of earth, air, water and fire in a very vivid way. Obviously colour plays an important part in Turner's work, particularly in capturing fire and sun, so try to find black-and-white reproductions. You will not get such vivid effects without colour, but you can achieve scenes with strong and dramatic contrasts. This should help you in your observations and studies of the elements and give you experience of using tone without the additional complications of introducing colour.

The projects should help you to become aware of these elements as physical entities, and suggest ways to represent them in a naturalistic way. The aim, also, is to give you an experience in the landscape that is essentially responsive to the forces of Nature.

STUDIES OF THE ELEMENTS

1-2 hours each drawing
Materials: *sketchbook (no bigger than A4), pencils, pencil sharpener, graphite sticks, charcoal, inks, dip pens, water-based felt-tip pens, erasers, water and containers, cotton wool, any other materials you feel are appropriate*

This project concentrates on the four elements of air, water, fire and earth. The drawings should be made from observations of different states that the landscape implies, using the appropriate materials for the different subjects. Many artists have made studies of this type as a way of collecting visual information on, and becoming aware of, the potential in the subject.

Atmosphere

These studies deal with the effects of light and atmosphere. This element is constantly changing, and the resulting drawings will probably be very dramatic and moody. Choose a landscape that contains space and distance. If it is practical to do so, select a remote area that has not been ordered by human activity, such as moorland or a heath. If possible, make your studies of atmosphere on a day when the weather is overcast. When doing this type of drawing, it is best if the elements are at their most extreme. If they are not, do not hesitate to exaggerate.

The first step is to understand the air, or atmosphere, as something

Right: A study of atmosphere

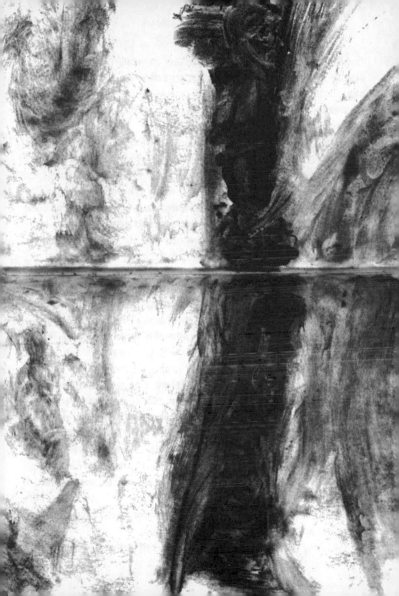

tangible. Atmosphere is not solid, and unless the weather conditions are extreme it is not opaque. It is also not stationary. We are not talking here about clouds, which can be dense and opaque; by atmosphere is meant the air between you and the next solid object or objects. How do you go about drawing something that is so transitory?

In the attempt to understand what atmosphere is, you will need to try out different materials. Atmosphere is continually changing, so you need to be able to push your material around the paper. Choose a medium that can be easily applied to the paper and just as easily removed. The drawing should be fluid, and have no suggested state of permanence. Start your observations by squinting your eyes, which helps to define the changing nature of light. It is this transitory scene that you want to depict. The drawing must be quick, spontaneous and responsive so that you can capture the continually changing conditions.

> *These studies are designed to allow you to find out what your materials can do and to experiment with them to create the effect of atmosphere. There are no hard-and-fast rules for making this type of drawing; it is a process of learning by doing.*

One method is to start by laying down all the dark or black areas first with charcoal, so that you have a black-and-white drawing. Do not draw the landscape with line, as this will impede your work. With a cloth or your hand, lightly smudge the drawing, making all the white areas grey. You might at this point need to re-establish the dark areas. You should now be able to recognise the beginnings of atmosphere in the drawing. Next, establish the light areas with an eraser, rubbing out what you see as light. Push and move this tone around the paper like the air that moves, establishing and re-establishing the lights and darks until you feel happy with the drawing. At some points in the drawing you will need to create heavier or thinner veils of air that appear to be moving over the landscape.

Any of the materials listed for this project could be used, and you should experiment with as many as possible. Mud and water applied with the hands can be very successful at capturing atmosphere. When using charcoal, pencil and graphite stick, your eraser is the vehicle that allows you to move your medium around the picture surface to create this atmospheric transience. When using inks, dip pens and water-based felt-tip pens, water has the same function. You can apply water using cotton wool to dilute the inks and felt-tip pens in order to create thinner veils of air and atmosphere where you want them.

Be prepared to experiment extensively with all these materials, pushing their possibilities quite physically, even to the point where you might tear the paper, in order to create a range of effects.

Water

Water occurs within the landscape in a number of different forms, such as lakes, rivers, streams, the sea or rain. Make a number of studies of these different manifestations of water.

The water in a lake can have different characteristics depending on the circumstances. For instance, the water could be choppy and rough, or it could be still and calm. Each condition needs to be observed and drawn. A calm surface will reflect objects by the lakeside and those, such as boats, floating on the surface, and these reflections might be distorted by a ripple. In choppy or rough water, the characteristics are very different as the water has a surge to it, and this in turn implies movement and direction.

The sea is another form of water. It has some characteristics similar to a large lake, but it is more extreme in its moods, and more violent and powerful. It can be dark, with waves crashing against rocks; or tranquil and gentle, lapping against a sandy shore.

A stream or river has different characteristics altogether. In places a stream may meander along its way. At other times it may suddenly rush over a fall of rocks, coming instantly to life, only to become calm again just as quickly. Of course, this all depends on other conditions. If there has

A study of water

been a lot of rain recently, the stream will probably become a torrent of fast, running water that is out of control; there may even be flooding. A stream eventually becomes a river, and this has different characteristics again. Although both a river and stream are constantly moving, a river is generally more predictable, except in extreme conditions.

Rain is another manifestation of water in the landscape. If you are sitting in a landscape looking across to the furthest distance, you may observe rainfall over part of it. Rain is a particular type of occurrence and it has particular characteristics. For example, it is drawn downwards by gravity. Rain may be a gentle drizzle or a heavy torrent blown by the wind across the landscape. It also sometimes has a transparent quality, like a veil descending over the landscape.

There are no rules for finding a visual equivalent for what we see and what we understand of a particular element. It might seem at first glance that this way of working — responding with materials emotionally to what you see and experience — would be relatively easy, but in fact it is not. At the same time as making your response, you have to understand intellectually the mechanics of your statement. You need the memory and experience of successful methods and drawings to use as a basis for further observations.

Fire

Fire might be caused by something burning in the landscape, or, more often, by the effects of a very strong sun. The sun can damage your eyes, so never look directly into it. When the sun is very strong, it makes the landscape appear crystal clear, creating sharp contrasts of light and dark. Because the sun can be damaging to look at, draw what you know of it, not relying just on what you see. Sunlight sometimes

You are drawing the effect of your observations and you are making a visual equivalent for what you see.

has a smouldering effect that creates a hazy atmosphere, particularly when it is shining through mist or thin cloud. This usually happens either in the early morning or late in the day when the sun is going down. Another effect of a strong sun is where it creates shafts of light through clouds or between trees in a forest or wood. Sunlight also varies depending on the season and country. Look at the way in which Turner captured the fire of sunlight, particularly sunsets, where the skies can appear to be on fire.

Earth

Earth is the land mass, and is affected by the other elements in one way or another. Mass is an expression of weight and form, in contrast to atmosphere and air, which are more ethereal. Mass is constant and needs to be modelled, in this case using tone. Choose a landscape that contains mountains, valleys, streams and lakes, or at least some of these.

> *Construct a tonal reading of the scene that endeavours to create the illusion of form and mass.*

It is important to gain a basic understanding of fundamental form and distance, as these are the foundations on which the other elements are usually imposed. Use line to create the basic layout by making a quick outline drawing showing where the main features of the landscape lie. Then create the idea of distance by observing the way the tone changes from the foreground to the background (illustrated overleaf). Usually it tends to be darker in the foreground and lighter in the background, although this is not always the case. You can then give the impression of mass by modelling using tone (see 'Classical Space', Project 1).

Make a number of drawings of all four elements so that you become familiar with the processes. This will put you in good stead for Project 2.

Left: A study of fire

65

PROJECT 2
THE LANDSCAPE DRAWING

4-5 hours
Materials: *A1/A2/A3 sketchbook/paper, drawing board if necessary, pencils, graphite sticks, charcoal, inks, dip pens, water-based felt-tip pens, erasers, water and containers, cotton wool, any other materials you think are appropriate*

The aim of this project (illustrated overleaf) is to do a drawing that gives a more complete picture of the landscape, using the experience gained from doing the studies. First, plot the composition on paper, making a quick outline drawing showing where the main features of the landscape lie. Then you can create the idea of distance by observing the way the tones change from foreground to background. You can then give the impression of mass by modelling using tone.

Once you have laid down the basic foundation for the drawing and described the space and form, begin to work over this. Observe how the other elements affect the underdrawing. For instance, there might be rain falling over a part of the landscape, obliterating some of the far distance. Mist might make the view very soft and hazy, and so on. This is a responsive drawing, but try to maintain the freshness of approach of the studies.

Left: A study of earth
Overleaf: A complete landscape drawing

> *Do not assume that you know how to draw something; approach each element in the spirit of gaining more knowledge and understanding of your subject.*

CHAPTER 6

EXPRESSIONISM

Expressionism has its roots in our feelings and emotional responses, and these are influenced either by what we see and experience, or from within, or a combination of the two. The intention in the previous projects was to record Nature, and at the same time to capture reactions of awe or serenity but without particularly focussing on them, drawing from observation, but allowing feelings for the scene to influence the drawing, even if on an unconscious level. This is one basis for an expressive piece of work. To take the process a stage further, the subject can evoke an emotional response, and that response becomes the dominating force in the work. In Vincent van Gogh's early work, the landscape is heavy, cold and brittle, whereas in the later drawings it has a lighter, more celebratory, rhythmical and optimistic warmth. Van Gogh was obviously affected by two very different landscapes and climates, the cold winter of northern Europe and the warm, more picturesque landscape of southern France. Although they work on other levels too, these are expressive drawings.

In this chapter we shall explore three different ways of creating an expressive drawing. The first starts from the eye, drawing from observation with an external stimulus for the work. This will be a development of the approach in the previous chapter.

The second project starts from the heart. You will be imposing your innermost emotions on the scene, using the scene as a vehicle for your feelings, unlike the first approach, in which the emphasis is on the external world. Often the feelings that we express are to do with our anxieties, so these works have a tendency to be on the more depressive side of our nature. Look at the seascapes of Emile Nolde (1867-1956), the landscapes of Edvard Munch (1863-1944) and the work of Chaim Soutine (1893-1943). In creating this type of work, you have to expose that innermost state, and this is not an easy thing to do. This type of work can fail tragically. You cannot just spill out a series of marks, tones or whatever to act as an expression of how you feel and then link it to the subject. You have to fuse the creative act with your knowledge of other drawing skills in order to make the drawing work from an aesthetic and compositional point of view. At the same time, those skills should not get in the way of a personal, creative act or statement. It is at this point that you begin to find your own voice and originate your own way of working.

The third project consists of constructed fantasy landscapes. These are an expression of something that is developed out of the mind rather than the heart. Look at the invented landscapes of Max Ernst.

Although each project concentrates on one approach – observation, emotion or intellect – they all have some crossover with the other two.

PROJECT 1
EXPRESSION FROM OBSERVATION

One 3-4 hour drawing
Materials: *your choice*

This project deals with the emotion that you first feel when you are confronted with a dramatic and inspiring landscape. Although it may appear very similar to the projects in the previous chapter, there are subtle differences. In this project you are responding in an emotional way to your observations of the landscape. It is not an easy project to direct, as we all feel very differently, and there is very little in terms of a procedure. Before you embark on the project, take a look at the landscape drawings of Frank Auerbach (b.1931), as they are a fine example of this type of work.

Draw intuitively and be prepared to take risks. Rely on your instincts for the first two hours, not questioning whether what you have done is good or bad. You can then begin to make value judgements on what you have done and rework the drawing. Do not be afraid to rework a drawing of this nature continually.

Be aware of precious areas in a piece of work. You can try to keep an area that you think is working well and alter everything around it, but sometimes you have to sacrifice these areas for the sake of a better overall drawing.

Above and below: Expression from observation

Exaggerate elements in the drawing, such as tone or line, or aspects of observed features, such as scale, proportions or depth of field. Because you are trying to come to terms with your feelings about what you see, your drawing will probably not be a representational record of the scene before you.

Be prepared for a difficult yet very rewarding drawing if you get it right. However, only you can be the judge of your own intentions, and that is the difficult part.

PROJECT 2
DRAWING FROM THE HEART

1-5 hours
Materials: *your choice*

The length of time you spend on this project can vary from drawing to drawing. Sometimes you must accept that you can do a very successful drawing very quickly, and that more time spent on a drawing will not necessarily produce a better one. You have to accept something for nothing, although at first you might feel some guilt about this.

The basic starting point for this drawing is the heart. With some people, their feelings are already burning inside them, waiting for the moment when they can make their escape, and generating an uncontrollable need to begin working. This can be a regular occurrence for some artists, but others experience gaps in their working life. This is quite natural. It is not easy to conjure up emotion if it does not lie just under the surface waiting to appear at a given moment, and you may have to wait until an appropriate time presents itself before attempting this way of working.

You may find this heartfelt way of working very difficult if your main source of stimulus is the eye or the mind. You may also be surprised by the type of drawings that you make. For example, not all happy people make happy drawings, and not all sad people make sad drawings. Sometimes the opposite happens; it could be that we compensate for how we are feeling at the time. When the time is right, you can approach the drawing by working from memory and using drawings from previous projects, or by working directly from the landscape.

Working from memory and other drawings
You will probably find that this is the best approach for this project because when you feel like producing a piece of work you do not need to draw directly

In the Western tradition, this type of drawing is usually placed in a conventional picture space However, it can be just as successful done in a flat, symbolic manner, as in the drawings of Paul Klee (1879-1940). Klee put images together in a very unorthodox way, yet they make a statement that is both expressive and symbolic.

Working from the heart

from the landscape. There is no set way of going about the drawing. Identify the type of emotion you want to describe, and use a previous drawing for the basic composition, which gives you a structure to work with.

Develop the drawing expressively, using your intuitive sense of mark-making. Let your feelings and emotions take the lead at this stage. It is not possible to say exactly how your drawing should develop, but one useful method is to exaggerate elements in the drawing, such as light, shadow, texture, space and scale, and to juxtapose and contrast elements in the landscape in order to express your ideas.

The next stage is to examine what you have produced and see how you feel about it. You may have made what you believe is a successful drawing. If so, that is fine; but be prepared to look at the drawing for some time before you make a final decision. It is generally better to change your mind at this stage and continue working, rather than coming back to it the next day, when you may have lost impetus. If the drawing is not satisfactory, think about why it is not working in the way you want, and then respond instinctively to your thought processes again. Repeat this procedure until you feel the drawing is finished. A great exponent of landscape work in this manner is the German artist Anselm Kiefer (b.1945), who has used a constructed landscape to unearth a whole history of emotions.

Working in the landscape

This approach is a fusion of observation and emotion, but with the emphasis on inner feelings, using the environment as the structure. The procedure is the same as in the previous drawing. A very good example is the contemporary British artist, John Virtue. His working process is quite unusual in that he works in the landscape on very large canvasses (about 4x3m/12x9 ft). He lays the canvas down in a field overlooking the chosen scene and then begins to let the work evolve.

Although there is a certain amount of recognition of the scene, you feel that the artist has created a type of performance on the canvas that is more to do with himself, his materials and the act of doing the work, rather than the scene in front of him.

PROJECT 3
CONSTRUCTING THE LANDSCAPE

Each drawing 12 hours over 2 days

This project consists of two drawings. The first is a fantasy landscape that is drawn from vegetables. For the second drawing you need to construct a small structure out of rubbish and make a drawing based on this.

Drawing I

Materials: *A0 paper, charcoal, eraser, masking tape, a selection of vegetables*

The aim is to create a drawing that has a strong mood, such as anxiety — in effect, a landscape of anxiety. This type of drawing is much more considered that those in the previous two projects, which is why it is referred to as an expression of the mind.

First, you need to get a selection of unusual vegetables, such as asparagus, broccoli, mushrooms, celery, ginger, chillies and any others that would be interesting. The idea is to place these in a constructed landscape, making their scale much larger than is natural, to create a mood of anxiety. Each vegetable should be drawn as a separate item, but placed in the context of a landscape space. So, on the A0 paper, create the space or environment for the vegetables to occupy. You can base this on a previous drawing, using the basic land mass rather than features such as trees and buildings. This should give you a barren, desert-like scene.

The next stage is to take one of the vegetables and set it up to draw from. Select a place for it in the drawing. If it is in the foreground, it should be quite large in scale. If you draw more than one of the same vegetable, make them smaller as they are placed further back in the landscape to emphasise the receding space. And draw the vegetable so that it sits convincingly in the space. For instance, you could make one appear from behind a hill. If you are unsure how to place the vegetables convincingly, look at your original drawing to see how features such as trees exist in the landscape. Approach this drawing using texture as a way of interpreting the scene (see 'Landscape Textures'), and remember to draw the space in between the objects, otherwise they will look like gaps in the drawing. Look again at the original drawing for this information.

Right: Constructing the landscape, Drawing 1

Drawing 2

Materials: *4 sheets of A1 paper, charcoal, eraser, masking tape, contact adhesive glue, 20x30cm (8x12 in) piece of board, household rubbish (see below)*

You should spend at least a morning constructing the landscape. Collect a number of small items such as polystyrene cups, scourers, packaging and so on, and cover the board with something textured. Glue the rubbish onto the board to make a landscape. When you have completed the construction, spray-paint it in black, as this will unify the colour and help in the drawing.

You are now going to draw a panoramic view from all four sides of the

Constructing the landscape, Drawing 2

structure, linking the drawings together. First, use an A1 sheet of paper in a landscape format (horizontal). Position the construction so that you are viewing it from one of the longer sides, and draw so that your drawing fills the paper. Use line to plot the composition, and complete the drawing with either texture or tone. If you use tone, illuminate the group with a directional light source. Then rotate the structure so that you are looking at one of the shorter sides. Attach a second sheet of A1 paper, in portrait format (upright), to the first with masking tape on the back, and draw this side in the same manner, linking the two drawings across the join. When you have finished the second side, rotate the structure again and draw the other long side in landscape format. Finally, draw the second short side in portrait format. Trim the portrait sheets if you wish.

When finished, you will have a long, panoramic view of the structure.

CONCLUSION

It should be clear by now that there is no one way to approach landscape drawing. Rather, after working through the different processes described in the projects, you should be able to begin to understand more clearly where your own strengths lie and what type of artist you are becoming. Some artists lean more towards the constructive side of the working process, starting from the mind, whereas others lean towards the emotional and expressive side. Others still take observation as their starting point.

It is not necessary to become adept at all three approaches in order to develop further. However, they are all present at some point in any drawing. Identify where your natural direction as an artist lies, and begin to develop that direction.

Published by Arcturus Publishing Limited
For Bookmart Limited
Registered Number 2372865
Trading as Bookmart Limited
Desford Road
Enderby
Leicester
LE9 5AD

This edition published 1996

Printed and bound in Great Britain

© Arcturus Publishing Limited/P. Stanyer, T. Rosenberg

ISBN 1 900032 75 9

Text: Peter Stanyer

Editor: Helen Douglas-Cooper
Design: Wilson Design Associates

ACKNOWLEDGEMENTS
The authors and publishers would like to thank the
following students for lending drawings for reproduction:
Rowena Blood, Philip Bodington, Jemima Broadbridge,
Tom Flint, Carol Grafham, Jane Johnson, Ian Johnstone,
Jeremy Linton, Sylvia Pizzinnato, Ruth Weinstock; and
thanks to all the students who donated drawings for
possible inclusion.

The authors would like to thank the City Literary
Institute and the Chelsea School of Art and Design,
where they teach many of these drawing programmes.